MW00761064

DEER

Sandie Lee Books

Thanks for checking out the Sandie Lee Books Series. Please note: All Rights Reserved. No part of this publication may be reproduced in any form or by any means, including scanning, photocopying, or otherwise without prior written permission of the copyright holder. Copyright ©
2014

Deer

The deer species has been around for millions of years. There is about 90 different species of the deer and they belong to the family of, Cervidae. Animals like the moose, elk and caribou are also a part of this family. Deer are considered ruminants. This means they chew their food, swallow it, then bring it back up to chew again - like a cow. In this article we are going to discover many more facts about the deer species. So let's get started.

Where in the World?

Did you know deer can be found in most areas of the world? The only places deer are not found are in Antarctica, South Africa, the Sahara desert and Australia. They can inhabit different regions and will live in wooded and forest areas, along with thickets, savannahs and prairie lands.

The Body of a Deer

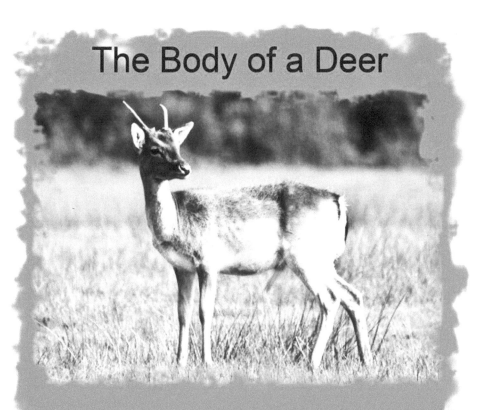

Did you know some species of deer can grow to be 300 pounds? Most deer have a brown coat. Their legs are very long and they have shorter tails. Each leg ends with a hoof. The body of the deer is quite stocky. They have longer necks, ears that stand straight up and a narrow muzzle.

A Deer's Antlers

Did you know the male deer has antlers and the female reindeer has them, too? Antlers are not horns. These bony formations grow from the deer's head. They can be very large and impressive. New antlers are covered in fine hairs called, velvet. After time, the soft velvet wears off.

What a Deer Eats

Did you know deer are herbivores? Most species of this animal eat leaves and foliage. Some also eat grasses, soft twigs. fungi, fruit and lichens. Deer can be very picky about what they eat. They also have a special bacteria that lives in their stomachs. This ferments the food and helps it to digest.

The Deer as Prey

Did you know deer are hunted by many different predators? The deer fall prey to many large carnivores like large cats, wolves and coyotes. Large species of crocodiles, alligators and snakes in the rainforest will also hunt and dine on deer. Man also hunts deer for its skin, meat, antlers and to use as trophies.

The Defense of a Deer

Did you know the deer is not totally defenseless? Deer will kick with their powerful legs and hooves to try and stop an attack. Male deer will fight each other by charging and locking their antlers. Deer try to avoid conflicts by running away. Deer are very fast and it takes a skilled predator to catch one

Deer Talk

Did you know deer can communicate through sounds? We may think deer go through life being silent, but they can actually make noise. When a deer is afraid it will grunt, snort and bawl. This animal will also make a bark-like sound when it is upset and a high-pitched whistle to attract a mate.

Mom Deer

Did you know the mother deer is called a doe and her baby is a fawn? The mother deer becomes pregnant in the fall time and will give birth in the spring - between 180 to 240 days. Some species of deer will give birth to twins. She gives birth lying down on her side and will lick her baby clean after it is born.

Baby Deer

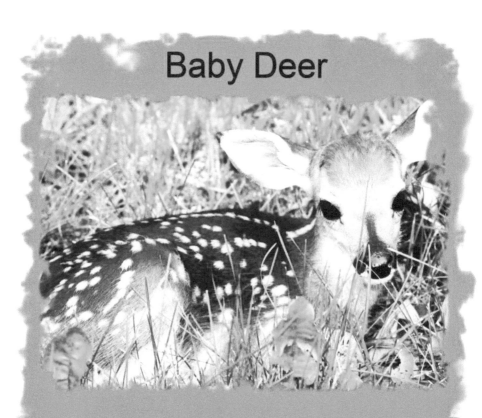

Did you know a fawn is born with white spots on its body? These spots keep the baby deer safe, by helping it blend in with its surroundings. The fawn can weigh from 4 to 8 pounds and will suckle milk from its mother. A fawn learns to stand and walk quickly after it is born.

Deer at Rest

Did you know deer take quick naps many times a day? Because deer have many predators, they doze for only minutes at a time. They have to be alert in case a predator is lurking. Deer like to lay on their stomachs with their front and back legs tucked under them to rest and to sleep.

Deer at Play

Did you know deer can play dead? When a baby deer is left alone, it may fake being dead if picked up. This helps keep it safe, especially from humans. Deer will also run, chase and kick when in playing-mode. Baby deers are more likely to engage in play.

Life of a Deer

Did you know deer live in groups called herds? In nature, deer will group together for protection from predators. They feed and travel as a herd. In the wild, a deer can live from 7 to 12 years-old. However, some deer in captivity have lived for as long as 20 years of age.

The Whitetail Deer

This species of deer may be the most recognizable. It is medium-sized, with brow grey or reddish colored fur. Its tail has white fur on the underside of it. The whitetail deer can grow to be up to 400 pounds! This deer is found throughout North and South America and as far as Peru.

The Fallow Deer

This deer species is common throughout Western Eurasia. It has a reddish-brown coat with white spots in the summer. The spots turn darker in the winter months. This deer can grow up to be around 220 pounds. Their lifespan is from 12 to 16 years-old. They eat vegetation as their main diet.

Quiz

Question 1: What other animals are part of the deer family?

Answer 1: Caribou, elk and moose

Question 2: What are the antlers of a deer covered with?

Answer 2: A fine velvet-like fur

Question 3: What are the defenses of a deer?

Answer 3: Kicking, locking antlers with another male deer, running away

Question 4: What special protection is a baby deer born with?

Answer 4: A spotted body. This is called, camouflage

Question 5: How many years can deer live in the wild?

Answer 5: It can live from 7 to 12 years of age

Thank you for checking out another addition from Sandie Lee Books! Make sure to check out Amazon.com for many other great titles.

CPSIA information can be obtained
at www.ICGtesting.com
Printed in the USA
LVHW071322161120
671787LV00078B/260

9 781494 999186